VICTORY
IN THE KITCHEN

VICTORY
IN THE
KITCHEN
Wartime Recipes

With an Introduction
by Laura Clouting,
IWM Historian

Published by IWM, Lambeth Road, London SE1 6HZ
iwm.org.uk

ISBN 978-1-904897-46-0

A catalogue record for this book is available from the British Library
Printed and bound in the UK by Gomer Press

10 9 8 7 6 5 4 3 2 1

Front cover image adapted from poster
A Clear Plate Means a Clear Conscience
(IWM PST 2814)

Design by Adrian Hunt

CONTENTS

INTRODUCTION

T HE SECOND WORLD WAR had a huge impact on the kitchens, and the stomachs, of millions of British people. This isn't so surprising when considering the context – this global conflict of unsurpassed destruction required all of a nation's resources to fight it and, in the words of the British government, food was 'a munition of war' (see poster on p.66). Without it, military forces could not fight on. Civilian workers could not contribute to their nation's 'war machine' in the unrelenting production of weapons and equipment. Ordinary people living through a state of war on the home fronts had to be sustained. Food was their fuel.

Imports were essential to Britain. As an island, it relied upon raw materials and supplies being shipped in from other countries. But during the Second World War, the sea became a battleground as German submarines targeted ships carrying vital consignments bound for Britain. A fierce moral imperative was laid upon people not to waste imported food once it had arrived safely. Sailors' lives had been risked for it.

This wasn't a new scenario. During the First World War, although Britain managed to feed itself, it was obvious to everybody that the nation was enormously vulnerable to attacks on merchant shipping.

With supplies from abroad once again threatened during the Second World War, Britain needed to exploit more fully what could be grown and produced at home. A great push was made to cultivate land for food production. The drive for self-sufficiency resulted in one million tonnes of home-grown food being reaped at the height of the war. This 'Dig for Victory' campaign saw the government energetically encourage the conversion of parks, playing fields, railway embankments, flower beds and every possible slither of land into vegetable patches. Agriculture was mobilised at state level, including the creation of the Women's Land Army to replace male farm workers who had gone to fight. Having been volunteers at the war's beginning, 'Land Girls' were eventually conscripted from towns as well as rural locations. Their efforts remain synonymous with growing more food to increase Britain's resilience.

Growing more was only one side of Britain's strategy to weather wartime pressures on food. The burning issue of 'fair shares' had to be dealt with to avert a civil crisis that might pit the rich against the poor in competition for purchasing limited supplies. To protect against this, food rationing came into force on 8 January 1940. The Ministry of Food, established during the First World War, was resurrected to administer a system that today may stoke up visions of shortages and sacrifices. But rationing's purpose was in fact to distribute food evenly across the population, and to prevent shortages becoming a critical problem.

Ration books were sent out to the occupants of every household. This precious paperwork allowed a civilian to make the purchase of strictly limited quantities of rationed foodstuffs. The personal weekly allowances fluctuated throughout the war, but the core idea was that ordinary people could plan meals around rationed items like meat, butter, cheese, sugar and even tea. These items were the dependable basis of lunches and dinners across the land.

The experience of shopping for food was transformed as people registered at local shops, from where they were now required to purchase their rationed foodstuffs. A free market remained for everything else, with customers left to slog it out for opportunistic purchases of non-rationed items like fruit. Exhausting queues became a hallmark of daily life. A black market of rationed goods thrived in some quarters, with heavy penalties for buyer and seller. Even sharing rationed goods beyond the household was technically banned, but friends and extended family persisted in donating rationed preserved fruit for wedding cakes.

The Ministry of Food had another vital purpose beyond encouraging self-sufficiency and administering rations. It had to inspire an inventive spirit in the kitchen to stretch supplies to the limit. The restrictions had the potential to irritate millions of people now bound to a limited diet, and fears of dietary tedium ran high. To combat this, unusual – and not always the most instinctively appealing – combinations of rationed and non-rationed foods were publicised in the public information leaflets like those you will encounter in this book. Daily radio broadcasts and public demonstrations by popular cooks like Marguerite Patten also aimed to cajole and inspire – and occasionally hector.

There is no doubt that eating in wartime involved a spirit of sacrifice and tolerance, as substitutes for much-missed foods were enthusiastically espoused from on high. The recipes in this book advocate eggless cakes, honey as a sweetener, and 'mock' dishes imitating family favourites. For a population wedded to meat, non-rationed rabbit provided some consolation, and occasionally a vegetarian invention was successfully 'branded' and accepted – no more so than Lord Woolton's Pie. Named after the popular Minister of Food, this root vegetable pie was blended with oats, topped with a potato crust, and induced such levels of satisfaction that it became a wartime legend. The same could not be said of other adaptations of familiar staples. Although bread was not rationed in wartime, the wholemeal 'National Loaf' made people miss white bread badly.

When the Ministry of Food wasn't advocating new recipe ideas, it was advocating the public health benefits of the wartime diet. Vegetables were championed as the saviour of the wartime family. The Ministry of Food's colourful messaging championed food stuffs in playful ways. From 'Dr Carrot' to 'Potato Pete', there was sometimes a patronising edge. Although taste might have been compromised, health was boosted as people ate less fat and more fibre. The manner in which people ate and managed their kitchen was also the subject of direction from official channels. People were urged to consume only what they could manage. In most cases this wasn't difficult, as excesses of food simply didn't exist for most. Even washing-up was considered a subject worthy of official comment. Official advice was to clean dishes just once or twice a day in 'big batches' to save fuel.

The archives of Imperial War Museums (IWM) are testament to wartime state intervention in the kitchen. By actively making use of the recipes in this book, you can literally recreate this history for yourself, and gain a sense of what culinary triumphs were borne out of sacrifice and hardship. The recipes are curiosities in some cases, and may even evoke shudders. Some are surprisingly delicious. Most of all, they reveal how invasively the war had intruded upon ordinary life in order to achieve the long aim of victory. The struggle to sustain the civilian population in the face of shortages continued beyond the war's end, and British people lived through further years of rationing and austerity in peacetime.

Few could argue against the Ministry of Food's grave responsibility to keep British people from hunger during the dangerous and nervous years of the war. However imperfectly executed, the emphasis on ensuring fair shares of food for everybody was a priority at the highest level in order to keep the home front going. The wealthiest were still able to purchase non-rationed food items – to an opulent extent in some cases. The very poor were used to sacrifices and struggles with food, and did not need to be told how to make the most of their supplies. But the principle of a level playing field and the benefits of diet to public health were regarded as both essential and welcome during the war.

By trying out some of these recipes, or even just by reading them, we can marvel at the tenacity with which people made the best of what was available to them. The ingredients might sometimes be at odds with twenty-first century tastes, and were a challenge to wartime taste buds too. But together with creativity and resourcefulness, these leaflets and posters helped people to think expansively and optimistically about food when it was scarce. This collection also serves as a compelling reminder about the seriousness of the subject. Food is far from frivolous. Britain was at war with waste in order to sustain its home front. The oft-used cliché of the kitchen as a battleground holds firm seven decades later.

Laura Clouting
Historian
IWM London

CONVERSION TABLES

Weights

Imperial	Metric
½ oz	10g
¾ oz	20g
1 oz	25g
1 ½ oz	40g
2 oz	50g
2 ½ oz	60g
3 oz	75g
3 ½ oz	90g
4 oz	110g
4 ½ oz	125g
5 oz	150g
6 oz	175g
7 oz	200g
8 oz (½ lb)	225g
9 oz	250g
10 oz	275g
12 oz (¾ lb)	350g
1 lb	450g
2 lb	900g
3 lb	1.35 kg

Liquids

Imperial	Metric
1 teaspoon	5 ml
1 tablespoon	15 ml
4 tablespoons	55 ml
¼ pint	150 ml
½ pint	275 ml
¾ pint	450 ml
1 pint	570 ml
2 pints	1.2 litres
8 pints	4.8 litres

Dimensions

Imperial	Metric
⅛ inch	3 mm
¼ inch	5 mm
½ inch	1 cm
¾ inch	2 cm
1 inch	2.5 cm
1 ¼ inch	3 cm
1 ½ inch	4 cm
1 ¾ inch	4.5 cm
2 inch	5 cm
2 ½ inch	6 cm
3 inch	7.5 cm
3 ½ inch	9 cm
4 inch	10 cm
5 inch	13 cm
5 ¼ inch	13.5 cm
6 inch	15 cm
6 ½ inch	16 cm
7 inch	18 cm
7 ½ inch	19 cm
8 inch	20 cm
9 inch	23 cm
9 ½ inch	24 cm
10 inch	25.5 cm
11 inch	28 cm
12 inch	30 cm

Cups

Cups	Imperial	Metric
1 cup flour	5oz	150g
1 cup caster/granulated sugar	8oz	225g
1 cup brown sugar	6oz	175g
1 cup butter/margarine/lard	8oz	225g
1 cup sultanas/raisins	7oz	200g
1 cup currants	5oz	150g
1 cup ground almonds	4oz	110g
1 cup golden syrup	12oz	350g
1 cup uncooked rice	7oz	200g
1 cup grated cheese	4oz	110g

1

STARTERS

'When salvage is all that remains of the joint
And there isn't a tin and you haven't a "point",
Instead of creating a dance and a ballad,
Just raid the allotment and dig up a salad!'

SWEDE SOUP

2 pints stock or water
1 ¼ lb swedes, peeled
   and shredded
2 oz onion, chopped
Salt and pepper to taste

2 level tablespoons flour
4 tablespoons milk
2 level tablespoons
   chopped parsley

Put the water or stock in a pan and bring to the boil. When boiling, add the shredded swedes, onion and seasoning. Boil for 20 minutes. Mix the flour to a smooth paste with a little water. Add to the soup and re-boil, stirring to prevent lumps. Cook for 5 minutes. Add the milk and re-heat but do not boil. Stir in the parsley just before serving.

LENTIL AND PARSLEY SOUP

2 oz lentils
½ oz leek or onion
4 oz carrots
2 oz sprouts (chopped)
1 pint water or
   household milk

½ oz fat
2 tablespoons chopped
   parsley
Salt and pepper

Wash and dice the vegetables. Fry the leek or onion and carrots in the fat, add the lentils, water and seasoning and simmer for 1 ½ hours. Sprinkle the chopped parsley and sprouts on the soup immediately before serving.

MOCK OYSTER SOUP

1–1 ½ lb fish trimmings
1 pint water
1 level teaspoon salt
1 blade mace
6 white peppercorns
1 clove
2 level teaspoons mixed
   herbs

1 small onion or leek,
   sliced (1 ½–2 oz)
8 oz artichokes
½ level teaspoon pepper
2 level tablespoons flour
¼ pint milk
Chopped parsley

Wash the fish and cook in the salted water with the mace, peppercorns, clove and mixed herbs in a muslin bag, and sliced onion or leek, for ½ hour. Strain off the stock and make up to ½ pint with water. Slice the artichokes and cook in the stock for ½ hour. Add the pepper, and sieve. Blend the flour with the milk, add to the soup and stir until it boils. Cook gently for a further 5 minutes. Sprinkle with the chopped parsley before serving.

STARTERS

19

POTATOES

feed without fattening and give

you *ENERGY*

SURPRISE POTATO BALLS

---

1 lb cooked potato
1 large carrot, grated
1 teaspoon chopped
   parsley
A little sweet pickle

Salt and pepper
A few teaspoons of milk,
   if necessary
Browned breadcrumbs

Cook the potatoes and beat them well with a fork.
Add the grated carrot, parsley, salt and pepper. Use a little
milk, if necessary, to bind the mixture, but do not make it
wet. Form into balls. Make a hole in each, drop in a small
spoonful of pickle and close the hole.

Roll in the breadcrumbs, place on a greased baking sheet,
and cover with a margarine paper. Bake in a really hot
oven for 15–20 minutes. Serve piping hot with good gravy.

SCOTCH EGGS

½ lb sausage meat
4 dried eggs reconstituted
   and hard-boiled

1 dried egg reconstituted
Browned breadcrumbs
Fat for frying

Divide the sausage meat into 4 portions. Flatten each
portion to make a circle about ½ inch thick. Place a
hard-boiled egg on each piece of sausage meat. Fold
over the meat to cover the egg completely. Dip in egg and
breadcrumbs, and fry in hot fat until golden brown. Serve
hot with gravy and greens, or cold with salad.

BAKED EGGS

PER PERSON:
1 egg
1 teaspoon milk

Salt and pepper
A little grated cheese
and butter

Grease individual ovenproof dishes. Break each egg separately and slide one into each dish. Sprinkle with salt and pepper and add 1 teaspoon milk. Place the dishes on a baking sheet, cover them and bake in a moderate oven until the eggs are set. Serve at once. A little grated cheese may be sprinkled over and a small piece of butter be put on each egg.

CHEESE AND EGG TARTLETS

Short pastry using
4 oz flour
2 oz breadcrumbs
1 ½ oz margarine, melted
1 egg, well beaten
2 oz grated cheese

1 level teaspoon baking
powder
5 tablespoons milk
and water
½ level teaspoon salt
Pinch of pepper

Line individual patty tins with the pastry. Mix the rest of the ingredients together and put a spoonful of the mixture in each pastry case. Bake in a hot oven for 20 minutes. This quantity makes 12 tartlets.

PARSNIP FRITTERS

---

2 large parsnips
3 small slices of stale
  bread
1 teaspoon flour

6 small pieces of bacon
Thick tomato sauce
Pepper and salt
Small piece of margarine

Boil the parsnips until tender. Drain and mash with margarine, pepper and salt. Roll bacon, thread on a skewer and grill. Shape the mashed parsnips into flat cakes with flour. Fry slices of bread and parsnip 'fritters'. Serve the fritters on the fried bread, previously cut into small shapes. The tomato sauce should be served separately.

SARDINE PUFFS

---

1 lb mashed potato
Salt and pepper to taste
A little flour

1 can sardines
2 teaspoons vinegar

Mix the potato with the seasoning and sufficient flour to bind into a dough which will roll out easily. Roll out and cut into rounds. Mash the sardines with the vinegar and place a little of this mixture on each round. Damp the edges, fold over and seal. Fry in a pan greased with the sardine oil and serve very hot.

6 STARS FROM the
WINTER GARDEN

SAVOY THE BIG-HEARTED TENOR ✶

KALE
THE EVER GREEN

SPINACH
THE STRONGEST MAN IN THE WORLD

THE **LEEKS**

THEY KNOW THEIR ONIONS

IF ITS HEALTH YOU'RE AFTER
CABBAGE
YOU LUCKY PEOPLE

THE **SPROUT**
SISTERS
Very tasty - very sweet

GROW THEM IN *your* WINTER GARDEN

MOCK LOBSTER SALAD

8 oz cooked white fish, free from skin and bone
5 level tablespoons thick salad dressing
1 ½ teaspoons Worcester sauce
1 level tablespoon tomato sauce
1 level teaspoon sugar
1–1 ½ level teaspoons salt
Pinch of pepper
1 ½ teaspoons vinegar
A little paprika pepper
A little finely chopped parsley
1 lettuce
Watercress, radishes, tomato or other salad

Flake the fish and mix with the other ingredients. Serve over the salad.

CABBAGE AND FRUIT SALAD

3 cups finely shredded cabbage
1 cup chopped apple
½ cup chopped ripe pear
1 tablespoon finely chopped onion
½ cup grated carrot
1 dessertspoon chopped mint
3–4 tablespoons salad dressing
Salt and pepper

Mix together the cabbage, apple, pear, onion, carrot and mint. Moisten with the salad dressing and add a little salt and pepper if necessary. Pile on to a dish and garnish with small sprigs of mint.

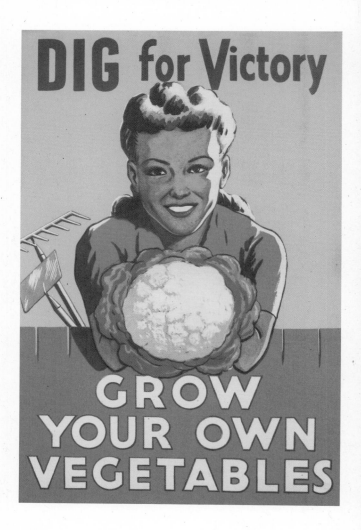

HORS D'OEUVRE SALAD

1 dried egg (scrambled)
1 teaspoon chopped herbs
2–3 lettuce leaves
2 tablespoons chopped
  cooked beetroot
1 sardine
Radish rose

2 tablespoons raw grated
  turnip
3 tablespoons cooked
  beans
2 tablespoons finely
  grated cheese

Mix the scrambled egg with the herbs and place on the lettuce leaves. Arrange the other ingredients in heaps around this. Other cooked or raw vegetables, mixed pickles and tomato roses may be used as alternatives. Serves one.

CARROT CROQUETTES

12 oz finely grated
  carrot, raw
6 oz finely grated potato,
  raw
4 oz grated cheese

1 ½ teaspoons salt
Pepper
½ teaspoon dry mustard
3 oz oatmeal

Mix the finely grated vegetables and cheese. Season, add the oatmeal to form a fairly stiff mixture. Form into croquettes and fry in hot fat.

A NEW FISH DISH

FRESH-
SALTED
COD

9^D lb.

2

MAINS

'Those who have the will to win
Cook potatoes in their skin,
Knowing that the sight of peelings,
Deeply hurts Lord Woolton's feelings.'

I'm a
*protective
food*

Says '**POTATO PETE**'

POTATO PIGLETS

---

6 medium well-scrubbed
  potatoes
6 skinned sausages

Cooked cabbage, lightly
  chopped

Remove a centre core, using an apple corer, from the
length of each potato, and stuff the cavity with sausage
meat. Bake in the usual way and arrange the piglets on a
bed of cooked cabbage. (The potato removed from each
is useful for soup.)

HAMBURGERS

8 oz minced beef
4 oz stale bread, soaked
  and squeezed
Pinch of herbs
2 teaspoons salt
¼ teaspoon pepper

¼ teaspoon mustard
4 teaspoons Worcester
  sauce
2 tablespoons chopped
  onion
1 egg (optional)

Mix all the ingredients together and form into 8 rounds. Fry in shallow fat for 15 minutes or until cooked in the middle. Put a large saucepan lid over the frying pan during cooking as this conserves the heat. Serve with potatoes and watercress or raw salad.

MOCK HAGGIS

2 teacups oatmeal
½ teacup bacon ends
  or hard fat
1 leek or onion
1 teaspoon salt

¼ teaspoon pepper
½ teaspoon bicarbonate
  of soda
Milk or pot liquor

Mix all the ingredients evenly and add sufficient milk or pot liquor to make a moderately stiff consistency. Put into a well-greased bowl or deep tin and steam for about 2½ hours. Serve with a good gravy, green vegetables and potatoes.

NOTE: To vary and increase nourishment add ¼ lb raw minced meat, or 2 oz liver, melt, ox kidney or lights.

For a healthy, happy job

Join the WOMEN'S LAND ARMY

For details: CLIVE UPTTON

APPLY TO NEAREST W.L.A. COUNTY OFFICE OR TO W.L.A. HEADQUARTERS 6 CHESHAM PLACE LONDON S.W.1
STREET

Issued by the Ministry of Agriculture and the Ministry of Labour and National Service

STUFFED OX HEART

1 ox heart (1 lb)

OATMEAL STUFFING:
*2 tablespoons medium
oatmeal or 4 tablespoons
national breadcrumbs*

*1 small leek or onion
(cooked)*
1 tablespoon melted fat
*¼ teaspoon mixed herbs
or 1 teaspoon chopped
parsley*

To make the stuffing:
Mix the ingredients and bind with the melted fat and a
little milk if necessary. To improve flavour, toast oatmeal in
a moderate oven before use.

Soak the heart in salt and water. Wash and cleanse
thoroughly; remove blood and cut off coarse fat and
skin. Fill the cavities of the heart with the stuffing and tie
up. Place in a covered baking tin with a little water and
dripping, and bake in a really hot oven for 15 minutes:
finish cooking very slowly for a long time basting
frequently. Time 2–2½ hours. Serve with brown gravy.

NOTE: Adopt a similar method for sheep's hearts.
Time for cooking ¾ to 1 hour.

MAINS

USE SPADES NOT SHIPS

GROW YOUR OWN FOOD
AND SUPPLY YOUR OWN COOKHOUSE

LAMB AND VEGETABLE RAGOUT

---

1 breast of lamb
1 onion
1 ½ lb finely diced carrots
1 ½ lb cabbage
1 pint water

½ oz sugar
1 level teaspoon ginger
2 level teaspoons salt
Pepper
2 oz flour

Trim off the fat and cut the lamb into neat portions. Dice onion and place with the meat in a large saucepan. Add water, pepper and salt and bring to boil. Cook gently for 1 hour. Add carrots and cook for a further hour and then put in shredded cabbage with a little extra salt. Cook till all is tender. Skim off surplus fat, and brown the flour and ginger in an ounce of it. Stir into the stew with the sugar, and season to taste.

LANCASHIRE HOT POT

---

6 oz scrag-end mutton
12 oz sliced carrots and turnips

8 oz sliced potato
Stock or vegetable water
Salt and pepper

Put the ingredients in layers in a casserole, finishing with a layer of potatoes. Season. Add stock to come half-way up casserole. Cover with greased paper and bake for 2 hours in a moderate oven.

RABBIT HOT POT

Bacon rinds or
  1 teaspoon fat
2 large carrots
3 or 4 potatoes

3 or 4 sticks celery
Cup of water
1 small rabbit

Melt the fat or frizzle the bacon rinds in a saucepan.
Add the prepared celery and fry without browning.
Add the remainder of the prepared vegetables, the water
and the seasoning. Cut the prepared rabbit into joints and
put on top of the vegetables. Cover with a well-fitting lid
and allow to stew 1–1 ½ hours according to the size of the
rabbit. Sprinkle with chopped parsley and serve very hot.

NOTE: Adopt this method for cooking tripe, brisket, ox
cheek, clod, lamb's tails and other cheap parts of meat.

MEAT CURRY

1 small onion
1 medium sized apple
1½ oz dripping
¾–1 lb beef or lamb
1½ tablespoons curry
    powder
4 tablespoons flour
¼ teaspoon dry mustard

¾ pint stock or water
1 teaspoon sugar
1 tablespoon chutney or
    vinegar
1 tablespoon marmalade
1 teaspoon black treacle
    or syrup
2 teaspoons salt

Chop the onion and the apple finely and fry in the melted dripping. Add the meat cut in 1-inch cubes and fry lightly. Remove the meat from the frying pan and work in the curry powder, flour and dry mustard. Cook for 2–3 minutes, add the liquid gradually and bring to the boil, stirring all the time. Add the sugar, chutney, marmalade, black treacle or syrup, and salt. Replace the meat and simmer for 1–1½ hours, or until tender. In place of rice, serve with macaroni, barley or potatoes.

BETTER POT-LUCK

with
Churchill
today

THAN HUMBLE PIE

under
Hitler
tomorrow

DON'T WASTE FOOD!

STEAK AND KIDNEY AND
BUTTER BEAN PIE

---

8 oz buttock steak
4 oz kidney
8 oz rough puff pastry
4 oz cooked butter beans

1 oz flour
¼ pint water
Seasoning

Slice the meat, dip it in seasoned flour and roll up with
a piece of kidney. Fill a pie dish with the meat rolls and
the cooked butter beans, adding water and covering the
pie with a fairly thick crust of rough puff pastry. Bake in
a hot oven, reducing the heat when the pastry is set.
Cook 1½–2 hours.

EGG AND BACON PIE

Short pastry using 6oz
  flour
2 eggs
2–3 oz bacon, chopped

1 oz fresh breadcrumbs
1 tablespoon milk
Salt and pepper to taste

Line a 7-inch flan ring or sandwich tin with two-thirds
of the pastry. Beat the eggs and mix in the bacon,
breadcrumbs, milk and seasoning. Pour into the flan case
and cover with the remaining pastry. Bake in a hot oven for
½ hour and serve hot or cold.

DEVILLED HERRINGS

3 level dessertspoons dry mustard
2 level tablespoons sugar
2 dessertspoons vinegar
4 herrings, cleaned and boned
4 level tablespoons chopped onion
1 bay leaf
6 cloves
½ oz margarine
5 tablespoons water

Mix the mustard and sugar to a paste with the vinegar. Open the herrings flat, spread the mustard mixture on the inside and roll up from the tail end. Fry the onion, bay leaf and cloves in the margarine in a saucepan until well browned. Add the rolled up herrings and the water, and cook very gently for 10 minutes. Baste the herrings occasionally with the liquid. When cooked, serve with sweet chutney.

FISH PASTIES

Suitable fish: Cod, coley, haddock, hake
Pastry using 6 oz flour
8 oz white fish, cut into cubes
4 oz cooked diced potato
1 level tablespoon chopped parsley
2 level tablespoons chopped onion
1 level teaspoon salt
¼ level teaspoon pepper

Roll the pastry into four 6-inch circles. Mix the fish with the other ingredients and pile a quarter of the mixture on each piece of pastry. Moisten the edges of the pastry and seal into a pasty shape. Bake in a hot oven for 30 minutes. Serve hot or cold with salad.

CURRIED COD

1 lb salted cod
1 tablespoon dripping
1 onion (small) or leek
1 tomato
1 apple or 1 tablespoon
  apple pulp
1 lb root vegetables

SAUCE:
1 tablespoon flour or 1 ½
  tablespoons national
  flour
½ tablespoon curry
  powder
2 breakfast cups fish,
  vegetable or other pot
  liquor

Tear skin from cod using a knife, wash thoroughly.
Place in a pan the skinned side down with just sufficient
cold water to cover and ½ teaspoon sugar to cover. Bring
slowly to boiling point, and allow to simmer 3 minutes.
Pour off the water. Remove bone and cut fish into slices
about ½ inch thick. Prepare vegetables, cut into thick
chunks. Melt dripping in a suitable pan. Add sliced onion
or leek, and fry lightly. Add sliced tomato, chopped apple,
curry powder and flour, and stir over the heat. Add the pot
liquor gradually and stir until boiling. Season with pepper.
Add the fish and vegetables and allow to cook steadily
for 45–60 minutes. Serve with potatoes or boiled rice,
if available.

Let your SHOPPING help our SHIPPING

PLAN YOUR MEALS TO AVOID WASTE

KEDGEREE

Suitable fish: Cod, hake, ling, any canned fish
1 onion, chopped
1 small bay leaf
½ oz dripping
1 level tablespoon flour

¼ pint liquid from the barley or rice
6 oz cooked pearl barley or rice
8 oz flaked fish
Juice of ½ lemon
Salt and pepper to taste

Fry the onion and bay leaf in the dripping until golden brown and work in the flour. Add the liquid and bring to the boil, stirring all the time; boil gently for 5 minutes. Add the barley or rice, fish and lemon juice and season to taste. Heat through and serve very hot, garnished with hard-boiled egg.

For curried kedgeree, add 1 level tablespoon curry powder to the onion and fry to a few minutes before adding the flour.

MAINS

43

MOCK GOOSE

---

1 lb salted cod
1 tablespoon flour or 1 ½
   tablespoons national
   flour
Pepper
1 tablespoon sage

1–2 onions or leeks
4–6 potatoes
1 cup water or pot liquor
2 tablespoons dripping
1 teaspoon vinegar

Tear skin from cod using a knife, wash thoroughly. Place in a pan the skinned side down with just sufficient cold water to cover and ½ teaspoon sugar. Bring slowly to boiling point and allow to simmer 3 minutes. Pour off the water. Remove bone and cut cod into convenient-sized pieces. Mix flour with pepper and sage. Slice onions or leeks finely; peel and slice potatoes. Dip the cod in the seasoned flour and arrange in layers in a dish or tin with the onions and potatoes, leaving a layer of potatoes on top. Add the pot liquor, dot with dripping, and bake in a moderate oven for ¾–1 hour.

Alternatively, heat the fat in a frying pan, arrange the ingredients as above, add the water, cover with a lid or plate, and cook steadily for ½–¾ hour. Brown underneath just before serving.

LORD WOOLTON PIE

FILLING:
1 lb seasonal vegetables
 such as potato, swede,
 cauliflower and carrot
3–4 spring onions

1 teaspoon vegetable
 extract
1 tablespoon oatmeal
Chopped parsley

Dice the vegetables and spring onions. Cook together with
the vegetable extract and oatmeal for 10 minutes with just
enough water to cover. Stir occasionally to prevent the
mixture from sticking. Allow to cool, put in a pie dish,
sprinkle with chopped parsley and cover with a crust of
potato or wheatmeal pastry. Bake in a moderate oven until
the pastry is nicely brown and serve hot with brown gravy.

PIE CRUST:
8 oz wheatmeal flour
1 level teaspoon baking
 powder
Pinch of salt

Pinch of powdered sage
 (optional)
¼ pint cold milk,
 or milk and water

Mix all the dry ingredients together. Stir in the milk, or
milk and water, and roll out the mixture.

VEGETABLE CASSEROLE
WITH DUMPLINGS

---

1 lb potatoes
½ lb carrots
A little chopped spring
onion
1 oz fat
1 quart of stock or water
1 level teaspoon mixed
herbs
1 level teaspoon chopped
parsley
Salt and pepper

DUMPLING MIXTURE:
2 oz fine oatmeal
2 oz plain flour
1 oz dripping or chopped
suet
Level teaspoon finely
chopped parsley
Pinch of mixed herbs
Pinch of baking powder
Cold water to mix

Scrub and grate the potatoes and carrots (do not scrape them), finely chop the onion. Heat the fat in a saucepan, add the vegetables and stir them over a low flame for a few minutes. Add the water or stock, herbs and chopped parsley. Season with salt and pepper, and simmer gently for 15–20 minutes, stirring frequently.

To make a supper meal – make a few savoury dumplings to cook in the stew. Sift the flour with a small pinch of salt and rub in the soft fat if it is to be used. Then add the oatmeal, seasonings, herbs, etc., and if chopped suet is used in place of dripping, it should be added now. Mix to a firm dough with cold water, divide into eight pieces and form into balls with floured fingers. Add these to the casserole about half and hour before it is to be served, cooking with the lid in position throughout.

EGG AND LEEK PIE WITH CHEESE PASTRY

PASTRY:
6 oz flour
Salt
1 oz fat
2 oz grated cheese
Water to mix

FILLING:
½ lb leeks weighed after
   prepping
Salt and pepper
4 dried eggs
   reconstituted

Boil the leeks in a very little salted water. Drain and chop. Mix flour and salt, and rub in the fat. Add the grated cheese and mix to a stiff dough with a little cold water. Divide into two and roll one half to fit a 7-inch diameter tin or plate. Mix leeks, salt, pepper and eggs. Pour into pastry case, and cover with a second piece of pastry. Bake in a hot oven for 30 minutes.

LENTIL CUTLETS

4 oz lentils
½ pint water
2 oz cheese, grated
1 small onion, grated
3 oz breadcrumbs

Salt and pepper to taste
¼ level teaspoon dry
   mustard
Fat for frying

Wash the lentils and cook in the water until tender and dry. Mash well and add the other ingredients. Shape into cutlets on a floured board and fry in a little hot fat until golden brown all over. Serve hot with tomatoes and brown gravy.

ONION, TOMATO AND HARICOT BAKE

4 oz haricot beans
1 lb onions
2 oz flour
½ pint milk
½ pint onion water
2 oz grated cheese

2 level teaspoons salt
½ level teaspoon pepper
¼ teaspoon dry mustard
8 oz sliced or bottled
  tomatoes

Wash the beans and soak overnight; cook until tender and drain. Peel, cut up and boil the onions until tender; strain and save the liquor. Make a sauce with the flour, milk and onion water, and add the grated cheese and seasoning. Arrange the onions, tomatoes and beans in layers in a pie dish (2 pint size), cover with the sauce and bake in a hot oven for 15–20 minutes.

3

PUDDINGS

'Reflect, whenever you indulge
It is not beautiful to bulge
A large, untidy corporation
Is far from helpful to the Nation'

A clear plate
means
A clear conscience

Don't take more than you can eat

BAKED JAM SPONGE

1 ½ tablespoons
  margarine or cooking fat
1 ½ tablespoons sugar
3 tablespoons finely
  grated raw carrot
6 tablespoons self-raising
  flour or plain flour and

½ teaspoon baking
  powder
3–4 tablespoons jam
  (fresh fruit pulp will do
  just as well in summer
  time)

Cream together the fat and sugar. Beat in the carrot, then lightly add the flour. Moisten to a creamy consistency with milk, or milk and water.

Spread half the jam or fruit in the bottom of a greased pie dish, pour in the pudding mixture and spread it evenly. Bake in a moderate oven for 25 minutes. Just before serving spread the rest of the jam or fruit on the top and put back in the oven for 3–4 minutes.

GINGER PUDDING

1 ½ level tablespoons
  sugar (or 1 tablespoon
  syrup)
2 oz margarine
6 oz flour

1 level teaspoon ginger
1 level teaspoon baking
  powder
Milk and water

Cream fat and sugar. Mix together with the flour, baking powder and ginger. Add to the creamed fat and sugar. Mix to a soft consistency with liquid. Steam for 1 hour.

STEAMED DATE PUDDING

6 oz plain flour and 3
  level teaspoons baking
  powder, or 6 oz self-
  raising flour
¼ level teaspoon salt
2–3 oz chopped or
  shredded suet

4 oz dates, chopped
1 ½ level tablespoons
  sugar
1 beaten egg (optional)
Approx. ¼ pint milk
  and water to mix

Sift the flour, baking powder (if used) and salt, add the
suet, dates and sugar and mix well. Mix to a soft dropping
consistency with the egg and liquid and turn into a greased
basin (1 ½ pint size). Cover with greased paper and steam
for 1 ½ hours. Turn out and serve with a custard or syrup
sauce. Serves 4.

HONEYCOMB MOULD

2 level tablespoons
  gelatine
1 pint milk
2 eggs

1 ½ oz sugar
A few drops of vanilla
  essence

Dissolve the gelatine in the milk. Separate the yolks from
the whites of the eggs and beat the yolks with the sugar.
Add the milk gradually, return to the saucepan and cook
until thick, stirring all the time. Remove from the heat and
beat in the vanilla essence. Whisk the whites of the eggs
until stiff and fold into the mixture. Turn into a wetted
mould and allow to become cold and set.

MINISTRY of FOOD

HELP WIN THE WAR ON THE KITCHEN FRONT

ABOVE ALL AVOID WASTE

CHOCOLATE QUEEN'S PUDDING

2 oz breadcrumbs
A small knob margarine
1 level tablespoon sugar
½ pint milk
2 level tablespoons cocoa

8 level tablespoons jam
  or jelly
3 dried eggs reconstituted
1 teaspoon vanilla essence

Put the breadcrumbs, margarine and sugar into a basin.
Boil the milk, cocoa and half the jam, and pour it over
the breadcrumbs, stirring the mixture thoroughly. Cover
and allow to stand for ½ hour. Beat the eggs thoroughly,
spread a tablespoon of jam over the bottom of a greased
pie dish. Add eggs and vanilla essence to the breadcrumb
mixture. Pour the pudding into the pie dish and bake in a
moderately hot oven until set – about ½–¾ hour. Spread
the remaining jam on top and serve hot.

WARTIME CHOCOLATE PUDDING

2 cups flour
1 cup grated carrot
1 oz sugar
2 tablespoons golden syrup
1 teaspoon bicarbonate
  soda

1 teaspoon baking powder
1 heaped tablespoon cocoa
¼ pint milk
2 oz margarine
A little vanilla essence
Salt

Cream the margarine and sugar together and stir in
the grated carrot, syrup, fruit and the rest of the dry
ingredients. Add milk to mix to a fairly stiff consistency.
Put into a greased basin and steam for 2 hours.

BAKED CUSTARD

3 dried eggs reconstituted
½ pint milk
1 level tablespoon sugar
Flavouring

Beat the egg and sugar together very thoroughly. Boil the milk and pour it on the eggs gradually, stirring well all the time. Add the flavouring. Pour into a greased dish, place the dish in a shallow pan of water, hot or cold, allowing the water to come about halfway up the sides of the dish. Bake in a moderately hot oven until the custard is set, about 40 minutes.

NOTE: Bake the mixture as soon as it is mixed. Do not allow it to stand.

CHOCOLATE CUSTARD

Baked custard recipe, plus
2 level tablespoons cocoa
2 level tablespoons sugar

Mix cocoa with egg and sugar, continue as for normal baked custard.

DRIED FRUIT CUSTARD

Baked custard recipe minus sugar,
plus 4 oz dates, figs, prunes
Or baked custard recipe plus 2 oz dried fruit

FLUFFY CUSTARD TRIFLE

8 oz stale cake, cut in
fingers
8 oz fruit, stewed and
sweetened to taste
2 level tablespoons
cornflour or custard
powder

1 pint milk
2 eggs
2–3 level tablespoons
sugar
A little flavouring
essence, optional

Place the cake in a dish and cover with the stewed fruit.
Blend the cornflour or custard powder with a little of the
milk and bring the remainder to the boil. Pour on to the
blended mixture, return to the pan and bring to the boil,
stirring all the time; boil gently for 3 minutes and remove
from the heat. Separate the yolks from the whites of the
eggs, beat the yolks with the sugar and add to the custard
in a pan. Return to the heat and cook for a further 2–3
minutes, stirring all the time. Add the flavouring if used
and allow to cool. Whisk the whites very stiffly and fold
into the custard. Pour over the fruit and cake and serve
very cold.

LEMON MERINGUE PIE

Short pastry using
  4 oz flour
1 oz cornflour
Grated rind and juice of
  2 lemons made up with
  water to ½ pint
1 oz margarine

1–2 level tablespoons
  sugar
1 yolk of egg

MERINGUE:
1 white of egg
Pinch of cream of tartar
1 level tablespoon sugar

Line a greased 7-inch flan ring or sandwich tin with the pastry and bake blind. Blend the cornflour with the liquid, add the margarine and bring to the boil, stirring all the time; boil gently for 3 minutes. Remove from the heat and cool slightly. Beat the sugar and egg yolk together, add carefully to the cornflour mixture and pour into the flan case.

Mix the egg white and cream of tartar, whisk stiffly and fold in the sugar. Place on top of the filling and bake in a cool oven until the meringue is crisp but not browned.

LEMON FLUFF

----

1 oz cornflour
Grated rind and juice of
   2 lemons made up to ¾
   pint with water

2 eggs
2 oz sugar

Blend the cornflour with a little of the liquid, bring the remainder to the boil and pour on to the blended cornflour. Return to the pan and bring to the boil, stirring all the time; boil gently for 3 minutes and remove from the heat. Separate the yolks from the whites of the eggs and beat the yolks into the cornflour with the sugar. Return to the heat and cook gently for a further 3 minutes, stirring all the time. Allow to cool. Whisk the whites stiffly and fold into the lemon mixture. Serve very cold in individual glasses.

BLACKBERRY AND APPLE FLAN

----

4 oz pastry
1 ½ lb blackberries
1 large apple (peeled and
   cored)

2 oz sugar
½ pint water

Line a 6-inch or 7-inch sandwich tin with the pastry and bake blind. Slice the apple and mix with the blackberries; simmer in the water and sugar for about 5 minutes. Strain from the juice and arrange fruit in the flan case. When cold, the flan can be decorated with mock cream (see p.67).

SCRAP BREAD PUDDING

½ pint custard
4 oz stale bread soaked
  in cold water and
  squeezed thoroughly

4 teaspoons sugar
Few sultanas

Put the soaked bread into a greased dish and cover with the custard, fruit and sugar. Put a little fat on top if possible and bake in a moderate oven for about 25 minutes.

OHIO PUDDING

---

2 oz flour
2 level teaspoons baking
  powder
1 oz sugar
2½ oz raw grated carrot

4 oz raw grated potato
2 oz dried fruit
1 level teaspoon salt
1 level teaspoon
  bicarbonate of soda

Mix all the ingredients together. Put into a greased basin, cover with greased greaseproof paper, and steam for 2 hours.

DIG FOR... PLENTY

GROW FOOD
IN YOUR GARDEN
OR GET AN ALLOTMENT

ISSUED BY MINISTRY OF AGRICULTURE AND FISHERIES.

PRINTED FOR H.M. STATIONERY OFFICE BY JORDISON & CO.LT.LONDON & MIDDLESBROUGH.

SWEET POTATO PUDDING

---

8 oz sieved cooked
  potatoes
1 oz cooking fat
Level teaspoon salt, less
  if potatoes previously
  salted

1 egg
2 dessertspoons honey
2 sticks diced rhubarb, or
  any fruit in season

Mix all the ingredients together and beat well, turning
in the diced fruit last of all. Place in a fireproof dish, and
bake in a moderate oven for about ¾ hour.

QUICK RICE PUDDING

---

3 oz rice
1 pint water
2 oz sugar

5 level tablespoons
  household milk (dry)
Few drops vanilla

Wash rice, put into boiling water and cook till soft and
the water has almost evaporated. Mix the milk, sugar
and vanilla to a cream with a little water. Add to the rice.
Cook for 2–3 minutes, and serve hot or cold.

CURD TART

1 pint milk
1 dessertspoon rennet
short crust pastry using
  4 oz flour
2 oz margarine

2 oz sugar
1–2 beaten eggs
Pinch of nutmeg
Grated rind of 1 lemon
1 oz currants, optional

Warm the milk to blood heat in a saucepan, pour into a basin and stir in the rennet. Allow to set, then strain through muslin allowing to drip for at least 30 minutes. Line a 7-inch flan ring tin with the pastry. Cream the margarine and sugar together and add the egg gradually. Mix in the curds, nutmeg, lemon rind and currants and place the mixture in the pastry case. Bake in a moderate oven for 30–35 minutes.

MOCK CREAM

3 level tablespoons
  household milk
1 level teaspoon sugar

½ oz margarine
A little water

Put the dried milk into a bowl, add sugar and a little water, sufficient to make into a smooth cream when it has been well beaten. Add the margarine melted and a little flavouring if liked.

eat

Daily

EAT greens
FOR HEALTH

FEED RIGHT
TO FEEL RIGH

4

BAKING

'The Queen of Hearts said "no" to tarts,
"There's wheatmeal bread for Tea.
Each cream-gold slice
Is oh, so nice
And better far for me".'

GINGER BISCUITS

---

4 oz self-raising flour
1 level teaspoon sugar
½ level teaspoon ground
    ginger

1 ½ oz fat
1 tablespoon syrup

Mix the ginger and sugar with the flour, rub in the fats, mix in the syrup and knead until smooth. Make into a roll and cut into slices. This should make about a dozen biscuits. Bake in a flat tin in a moderate oven for 15–20 minutes or until pale brown.

HONEY OATMEAL COOKIES

---

8 oz medium oatmeal
1 oz coconut
½ small teaspoon salt

3 oz margarine
1 large tablespoon honey

Warm the margarine until soft, then cream it with the honey. Knead in the oatmeal and coconut and the salt. Knead well until it binds together. Roll into balls and put on to a prepared baking sheet. Press slightly to flatten each ball and bake in a slow oven ½–¾ hour.

FRUIT SHORTCAKE

2 oz margarine
6 oz plain flour and 3
  level teaspoons baking
  OR
  6 oz self-raising flour
2 oz sugar

2 tablespoons water
2 level tablespoons flour
¼ pint juice from the
  stewed fruit
¾–1 lb fruit, stewed and
  sweetened to taste

Rub the margarine into the flour and baking powder, if used; add the sugar and mix to a very stiff dough with the water. Press into a 7-inch flan tin and bake in a moderate oven for 25–30 minutes. Blend the flour with the fruit juice and bring to the boil, stirring all the time; boil gently for 5 minutes. Stir in the fruit and leave to cool. Pile the fruit mixture over the shortcake base.

CARROT CAKE

6 oz flour
1 level teaspoon baking
  powder
3 oz fat
3 oz oatmeal
3 tablespoons raw
  grated carrot

1 ½ tablespoons sugar
1 tablespoon dried fruit
1 dried egg
  (reconstituted)
1 dessertspoon syrup
Water to mix

Rub fat into flour, add dry ingredients and carrots and mix thoroughly. Add the syrup, reconstituted egg, and sufficient water to form a fairly stiff consistency. Place in a greased tin and bake in a moderate oven for 1 hour.

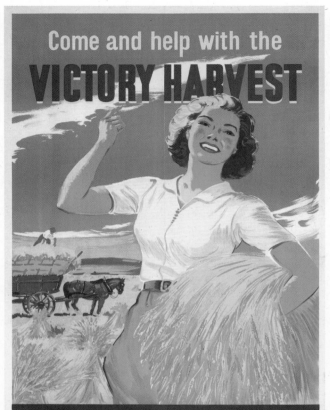

Come and help with the
VICTORY HARVEST

You are needed in the fields !

APPLY TO NEAREST EMPLOYMENT EXCHANGE FOR LEAFLET & ENROLMENT FORM
OR WRITE DIRECT TO THE DEPARTMENT OF AGRICULTURE FOR SCOTLAND
15 GROSVENOR STREET, EDINBURGH.

EGGLESS FRUIT CAKE

8 oz self-raising flour
½ level teaspoon grated
  nutmeg
4 oz margarine
1 heaped tablespoon
  golden syrup
4–6 oz sultanas or
  currents (or mixed fruit)

Pinch of salt
½ level teaspoon
  mixed spice
2 oz sugar
½ level teaspoon
  bicarbonate of soda
¼ pint hot water

Sieve the flour, nutmeg, spice and salt together. Put the margarine, fruit, sugar and syrup with the water in a saucepan, and bring to the boil. Allow to simmer for 3 minutes. Cool, and add the bicarbonate of soda. Make a well in the centre of the flour etc., pour in the cooled mixture, stir quickly together, mixing well. Put into a 6-inch cake tin lined with greaseproof paper, and brushed with melted margarine, and bake for 1¼ hours on the middle shelf of a moderate oven. Cool on a wire tray.

DIG FOR VICTORY

EGGLESS STEAMED CHOCOLATE CAKE

5 oz plain flour
1 level tablespoon sugar
2 level tablespoons cocoa
2 level tablespoons baking powder

1 oz margarine
2 level tablespoons syrup
6 tablespoons milk, or milk and water

Mix the dry ingredients thoroughly and rub in the margarine. Slightly warm the syrup and milk, or milk and water, and add to the other ingredients. Beat until the consistency of batter. Pour into a greased 5-inch tin, cover with a piece of greased paper and steam for 1 hour. Do not cut the cake until the next day.

POTATO OVEN SCONES

6 oz plain flour
2 level teaspoons baking powder
½ teaspoon salt

4 oz mashed potato
4–5 tablespoons milk
1 oz fat

Sift the flour, salt and baking powder into a basin. Mix thoroughly with the potato. Rub the fat in with the tips of the fingers, and blend into a soft dough with the milk. Roll out to ½-inch thickness, cut into small rounds and glaze the tops with milk. Bake on greased baking sheets in a hot oven for 15 minutes.

your

NATIONAL

WHEATMEAL

BREAD

is here!

BROWN BREAD

---

3 ½ lb flour
1 oz yeast
1 ½ pints tepid water

3 ½ teaspoons salt
1 teaspoon castor sugar

Mix the salt and flour, and place in a warm basin in a hot place to heat slightly.

Cream the yeast and sugar together in a slightly warmed basin. The mixture should become liquid. Add the tepid water, which should be just the heat of your little finger. Make a well in the centre of the warm flour, pour in the liquid and sprinkle a little flour over it. This accelerates the growth of the yeast.

Cover the basin with a warm cloth and put to rise in a warm place for 20 minutes. Then mix the flour and yeast and knead until the dough is smooth and elastic. Put into a floured bowl and leave it covered in a warm place until it doubles in size.

Knead again. Divide the dough into four 1-lb loaves. Put them in a warm place until the required size is reached. Bake in a hot oven until the loaf is golden brown and sounds hollow if tapped underneath. Cooking time is about ¾–1 hour for a 1lb loaf.

CRUMPETS

1 lb 2 oz plain flour
¾ oz yeast or and ¾ oz
   dried yeast
1 level teaspoon sugar
5 level teaspoons salt

1 pint lukewarm water
¼ pint cold water
½ level teaspoon
   bicarbonate of soda

Blend the yeast with the sugar, and gradually stir in the lukewarm water. Sieve the flour, make a hole in the centre, pour in the yeast mixture, stir together until thoroughly mixed, cover, and leave in a warm temperature for 1½ hours. Blend the bicarbonate of soda smoothly with the ¼ pint of cold water. Add to the yeast and flour mixture, beating well. Leave to stand for 10 minutes longer in a warm place. Finally stir in the salt.

Grease the crumpet rings lightly, and place on a moderately hot non-greased girdle or hot plate. Ladle the batter into the rings, allowing about ⅛ of a pint (or 5 tablespoons) to each, and cook over a moderate heat until the surface is well covered with holes (8–10 minutes). Then remove the rings, turn and cook the other side. Serve hot, spread with margarine, or toast when cold, and spread with margarine. Makes 18 crumpets.

MUFFINS

14 oz plain flour
¾ oz yeast or dried yeast
2 ½ level teaspoons salt

½ pint lukewarm water
1 rounded teaspoon
sugar

Sieve the flour and salt together. Blend the yeast with the
sugar, and mix slowly with the lukewarm water. Add to
the flour, and mix to a smooth dough. Mix with a wooden
spoon for 5 minutes in a warm temperature. Cover the basin
with a cloth, and leave in a warm temperature for ¾ hour.

Knock back the dough to its original size. Cover again
with the cloth, and leave in a warm place for a further
¼ hour to rise again. Divide into 6 portions, mould into
rounds, and fit into greased muffin rings placed on a
lightly floured board. Leave to prove (or rise) in a warm
place, covered with a damp cloth, for 45–50 minutes.
Heat to a moderate temperature a lightly greased girdle or
hot-plate, and cook the muffins, still in the rings, for 5–7
minutes on each side. When one side is cooked, remove the
ring before turning over. Split open and serve either hot, or
toasted when cold, spread with margarine. Makes 6 muffins.

NOTE: The proving time varies according to temperature.
When ready for cooking, the surface of the muffins will
retain the impression of the finger when lightly pressed.

IMAGE LIST

All images © IWM unless otherwise stated. Every effort has been made to contact all copyright holders, the publishers will be glad to make good in future editions any error or omissions brought to their attention.

All recipes, illustrations and quotations taken from original Second World War Ministry of Food information leaflets.

p.6 (D 2374): A woman purchases some pancake mixture – 'no eggs required' – from a grocers during the Second World War.

p.8 (D 9617): Land girls harvest flax on a farm in Huntingdonshire, 1942.

p.10 (D 24990): Women and children queue to buy vegetables from a greengrocer in London, 1942.

p.12 (HU 36119): Allotment holders on Hampstead Heath, 1940.

16 (IWM PST 3448); 20 (IWM PST 3366); 24 (IWM PST 0671); 26 (IWM PST 16807); 28 (IWM PST 0068); 30 (IWM PST 20603); 32 (IWM PST 6078); 34 (IWM PST 6078); 36 (IWM PST 8105); 38 (IWM PST 3108); 42 (IWM PST 14757); 46 (IWM PST 0200); 50 (IWM PST 0102); 52 (IWM PST 2814); 54 (IWM PST 17435); 56 (IWM PST 20697); 62 (IWM PST 2893); 64 (IWM PST 20689); 66 (IWM PST 20687); 68 (IWM PST 3454); 72 (IWM PST 0146); 74 (IWM PST 0059).

ACKNOWLEDGEMENTS

With thanks to Laura Clouting, Caitlin Flynn, Madeleine James and the staff of IWM. Thanks also to Adrian Hunt for the design.